Organising Your Second Marriage

CAROLE CHAPMAN

foulsham

LONDON NEW YORK TORONTO SYDNEY

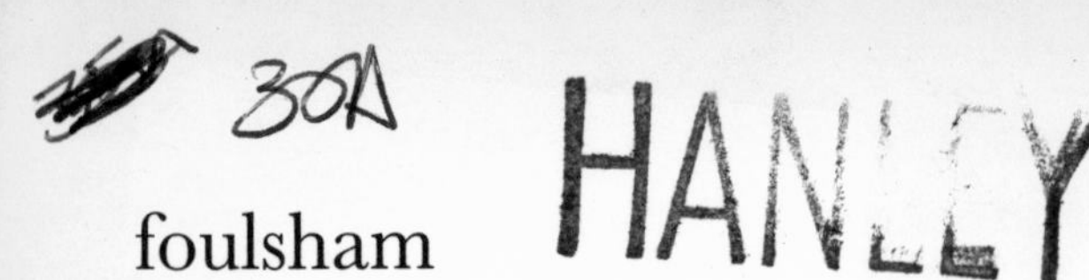

foulsham
Yeovil Road, Slough, Berkshire SL1 4JH

OTHER TITLES IN THE WEDDING COLLECTION:
The Complete Wedding Organiser and Record
The Complete Wedding Video Organiser
The Step-by-Step Wedding Planner
Your Guide to Planning the Wedding Day
The Best Man's Organiser
Wedding Speeches and Toasts
Getting it Right: Wedding Etiquette
Getting it Right: Your Wedding Planner
Getting it Right: The Best Best Man
Getting it Right: Wedding Speeches

DISCLAIMER
While every effort has been made to ensure the accuracy of all the information contained within this book, neither the author nor the publisher can be liable for any errors. In particular, since laws change from time to time, it is vital that each individual checks relevant legal details for themselves.

ISBN 0-572-01987-4

Designed and Typeset in Great Britain by Peter Constable Ltd.
Printed in Great Britain at Cox & Wyman Ltd, Reading.

Contents

Introduction

A new marriage marks a new beginning, so there is every reason to celebrate and since it is the first time you are marrying each other, you are entitled to have the type of wedding that suits your age and lifestyle. All weddings should be celebrated with joy, symbolising hope and happiness for everyone involved.

There are, no doubt, some people who still believe that no matter what the circumstances a second marriage should occur without celebration but you should not allow such views to ruin your plans and dissuade you from having the wedding of your dreams which will mark the start of your new life together.

This book makes suggestions for the marriage of women and men, irrespective of age, who have rediscovered love and who want to share their future lives together. Many concerns regarding second marriage, for example whether the bride should wear white and whether she should be attended, are addressed within this book and it is intended that the guidelines should not restrict but help make clear the procedures for all who participate whether you are a widow, widower, divorcee, or a member of the wedding party.

CHAPTER 1

Second Weddings

It is a fact that the number of remarriages have been and still are on the increase.

It is also true that second weddings used to be conducted as small private affairs and even today they are often more informal, quieter and less extravagant celebrations than first marriages especially if both partners are divorced, but they are still a time to celebrate a joyous occasion with family and friends. So, a second wedding can have all the fanfare of a first wedding and this is now more generally accepted.

While many aspects of a second wedding vary only slightly from a first, they are usually complicated by relationships with ex in-laws, children and those who have already celebrated (and given gifts) during the first wedding of either the bride or groom, or both.

When a man marries for the second time, wedding etiquette is almost exactly the same as for his first marriage but there are differences for a widow or divorcée who remarries and these are explained in the relevant chapters.

The marriage of a widower is much less restricted by

tradition than it is for a widow but nonetheless it is commonly less formal than a first wedding and decisions concerning the degree of formality, the service, the number of guests and scale of reception are generally made by the bride.

CHILDREN

It is vital that anyone entering into a second marriage realises that children from a first marriage always form a link with the past that should never be severed.

Children must have access to the parent they are no longer living with and similarly parents must have access to their children. The inevitable disruption that this will cause should not be ignored.

All sorts of problems can arise when step-children are living with a new partnership, for example the question as to whether they continue to behave as their parents saw fit or whether they should be expected to conform to new standards? Needless to say, resentment, jealousy, suspicion, regret and even hostility can flourish on both sides.

Both parent and child need the opportunity to spend time alone together. Children instinctively dislike change and need to be constantly reassured of the security of their future. Obviously, a step-parent wants to create a happy family unit but it is only natural that they are keen to make some changes especially in a home that was originally styled by a predecessor.

It is important for the new family to get together and discuss everyone's expectations of the future. A step-parent's role is often unclear and likewise the children do not know how to react. Patience, tact and mental strength are vital virtues on both sides. One very useful tip for step-parents is that they should never criticise a child's natural parents for obvious reasons.

Any couple's first consideration has to be their children and step-families come together with varying degrees of ease or difficulty, depending on the level of willingness of all parties to try to make it work. It should be remembered that the children of previous marriage have already experienced either divorce or the death of a parent and may well feel resentful and suspicious of any new start. Loyalties are very important to children and it is only natural that they will worry, especially if they are acquiring new brothers and sisters.

Children must be the first to learn of a parent's forthcoming marriage and need to be involved as much as possible in both the planning and preparations so that they feel part of future plans and commitments. Their participation should include some special responsibilities both before and on the wedding day.

It is the responsibility of the parent to make the news of a forthcoming marriage known to his or her children without the presence of the prospective new partner. The children then have the opportunity of expressing any anxieties they may have. The bride and groom should then talk to the children together, addressing their individual concerns and making clear to them definite and secure plans for their future.

Parents and step-parents need to realise that the merging of new relationships together with a new partnership is very difficult for any second marriage and consequently it is important to make allowances for this.

LIFE INSURANCE

Marriage in itself does not make life insurance necessary (although the family home must be covered in the event of one of the partner's dying). However, if there is a family, both partners should ensure that they are covered by life insurance for which it is worth assessing the level of income that the surviving partner and the children would need. Inevitably, there would be great financial loss to the family whichever partner dies. It is not simply a question of covering the potential loss of breadwinner's earnings, child minders and housekeepers also cost money!

FINANCIAL PLANNING

It is important to re-think financial affairs as the wedding approaches. As with the outset of married life, it is sensible to decide on the degree of financial independence that each partner will maintain and how best to take advantage of the new situation. If marrying a partner with a family for instance, financial priorities are likely to change yet again in order to reflect new responsibilities.

Whether married or single, everyone is now entitled to a personal allowance' (the amount of money earnable before paying tax). Married couples are allowed an extra small allowance. It may be useful to note that the tax year runs from 6 April to 5 April and if the wedding takes place before 6 May, the full allowance will be given. After this, one twelfth of the allowance will be awarded for each month of the year that the couple are married.

PRE-NUPTIAL AGREEMENTS

A pre-nuptial agreement is obviously a sensitive issue and many people feel that it reduces a relationship to pounds and pence or that it predetermines that a marriage is going to fail. However, such agreements are becoming more common.

The first step would be to seek the professional advice of a solicitor to check exactly how a pre-nuptial agreement is worded, what is usually included, how such an agreement ties in with the will, and how children and other family members would be affected by the disbursement of assets. Once the legal aspects are understood, these must be explained extremely tactfully to the future partner. A suggestion might be that the other partner has a similar agreement drawn up for dual protection.

JOINT ARRANGEMENTS

In addition to sorting out such legal and financial matters for the future, it will be necessary to decide whether to have joint or individual bank and/or building society accounts, who will contribute to daily living expenses, and how future educational costs for children will be covered.

It is far better to decide on these points together and in advance than to allow conflict affect relationships. It is interesting to note that next to children, legal and financial matters can create the biggest problems in second marriages, just as they do in first marriages.

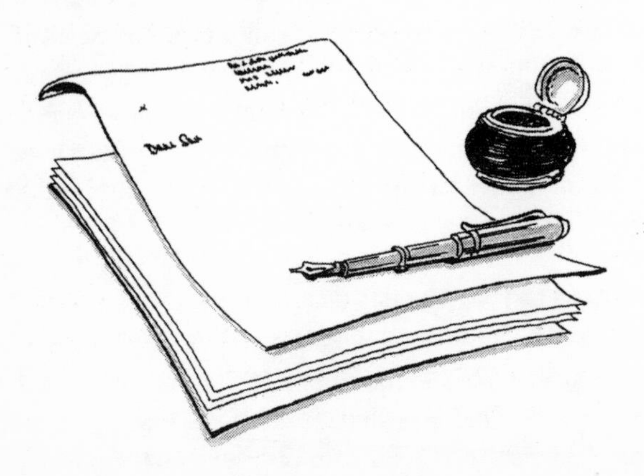

CHAPTER 2

Engagement

Sharing the news with the prospective bride's parents is something that can be done together unless it is felt that her parents would not be in favour of the marriage, in which case the bride should do the communicating unassisted by the groom. Being frank with both sets of parents is obviously the best advice.

If there are children from a previous marriage, then they should be the first to discover the news as the impending changes will have a greater impact on them than on the parents of the couple getting married. It is important that the children hear the news directly, not indirectly from a grandparent or other relative. The parents should then be informed immediately, again so that they learn of the news directly and not from the children or anyone else. An ex-spouse should be informed directly after the children are told.

For the couple who each have grown families of their own, it is still appropriate that the children are informed personally by their parent rather than indirectly. There really is no need to set the stage for all the children to become good friends, which of course they may not! However, if they are to be present at the wedding it may be appropriate to have a small gathering beforehand at which they can be introduced to one another, after they have had the opportunity to get accustomed to the idea of the marriage.

ANNOUNCEMENTS

An announcement of an engagement should be made only when both members of the couple are legally free to marry someone else, no matter how close the scheduled wedding date.

Informal

Informal announcements may be made personally, by letter or by telephone.

The following list may be useful for making sure that no one is forgotten.

INFORMAL ANNOUNCEMENTS

Name	*Address*	*Telephone*	*Done* ✓

INFORMAL ANNOUNCEMENTS *continued*

Name	*Address*	*Telephone*	*Done* ✓

Formal

It is perfectly in order to announce an engagement in the newspaper to share the happy news with friends and acquaintances. It used to be the case that a woman over the age of forty did not announce her engagement in the newspaper for either her first or second marriage. Instead, she would telephone or write to her relatives and friends. With the increase in the number of couples marrying later in life and the increasing number of second marriages, this tradition is no longer followed.

It would not be appropriate to send an announcement to the newspaper when there has recently been a death in either family or when a close family member is seriously ill. Instead, the announcement may be made public some time later.

As for a first marriage, the bride's mother may send an announcement to the local press.

If one of the prospective bride's parents is deceased, the name of the deceased parent should be mentioned in the wording of the announcement:

Mr/Mrs Ned/Nancy North
announces the engagement of
his/her daughter
Nel
to
Mr Sam South
son of Mr and Mrs Sid South
Nel is also the daughter of
the late Ned/Nancy North
....

If one of the prospective groom's parents is deceased, the form differs slightly:

Mr and Mrs Ned North
announce the engagement of
their daughter
Nel
to
Mr Sam South
son of Mrs Samantha South
and the late Mr Simon South
......

Children may also make the announcement:

The engagement of
Mrs Nel North
of Northton
to
Mr Sam South of Southton
has been announced
......

Or

The sons of
Mrs Nel North
of Northton
have announced
Mrs North's engagement
to Mr Sam South
......

If the mother is a divorcée, her first name would be used:

Mrs Nel North

If the mother is a widow, her deceased husband's name would be used:

Mrs Ned North

SETTING THE DATE

Marriages in register offices may take place on any day except Christmas Day, Good Friday and Sundays; they are generally not allowed in churches on Sundays.

The date of the wedding depends on the length of the engagement, work commitments, family diaries, honeymoon dates and seasonal weather.

Late Spring used to be the most popular season for weddings because there were tax advantages. Many couples still favour this time in order to take advantage of lower priced off-season holiday deals. Summer weddings are also popular so that the honeymoon coincides with the annual Summer holiday. The least popular time for large weddings is late Winter, making this a good time for the smaller weddings in register offices.

SETTING THE DATE

WEDDING

Day

Date

Time

AVAILABILITY OF:

Best Man

Maid/ Matron of Honour

Parents: Bride's

Groom's

Church/Register Office

HONEYMOON

Dates From To

Notes

CHAPTER 3

Legal Requirements

THE CEREMONY

In England and Wales, a marriage must be solemnised by an authorised person, such as:-

- the registrar of any register office

- ordained ministers of the Church of England

- ministers of other religious denominations who have been legally authorised to register marriages.

SEX

In the UK, one partner must have been born male and the other female.

MINIMUM AGE

Both partners must be over the age of 16. However, someone between the ages of 16 and 18 who has been widowed or divorced does not need parental consent.

WITNESSES

The parties to the marriage must arrange for the

attendance of two witnesses to be present at the marriage and to sign the register.

TIMING

The hours between which weddings may take place are 8 am and 6 pm.

RELATIONS WHO MAY NOT MARRY

The prohibited marriages are those of close family or blood relatives.

A man may not marry his:

Mother
Adoptive mother or former adoptive mother
Daughter
Adoptive daughter or former adoptive daughter
Father's mother
Mother's mother
Son's daughter
Daughter's daughter
Sister
Father's sister
Mother's sister
Brother's daughter
Sister's daughter
Wife's mother
Wife's daughter
Father's wife
Son's wife
Father's father's wife
Mother's father's wife
Wife's father's mother
Wife's mother's mother
Wife's son's daughter
Wife's daughter's daughter

Son's son's wife
Daughter's son's wife

A *woman may not marry her:*

Father
Adoptive father or former adoptive father
Son
Adoptive son or former adoptive son
Father's father
Mother's father
Son's son
Daughter's son
Brother
Father's brother
Mother's brother
Brother's son
Sister's son
Husband's father
Husband's son
Mother's husband
Daughter's husband
Father's mother's husband
Mother's mother's husband
Husband's father's father
Husband's mother's father
Husband's son's son
Husband's daughter's son
Son's daughter's husband
Daughter's daughter's husband

"Brother" and "sister" include half-brothers and half-sisters.

It is legal, however, for the following to marry:

A man may marry his/the:
Brother's widow
Dead wife's sister
Sister of ex-spouse

A woman may marry her/the:
Sister's widower
Dead husband's brother
Brother of ex-spouse

For the latter categories, namely divorced persons, it is almost certain that the minister will still refuse to perform the ceremony. The alternative is to marry in a register office where no objections will be raised.

If there is any doubt about the marriage of relations or divorced persons, the minister or Superintendent Registrar should be consulted as soon as possible.

SECOND MARRIAGES

No person who is already married to a living spouse should marry someone else; if they do so, the second marriage is invalid.

No person who is going through a divorce may marry until the Decree Absolute has been granted.

There is no limit to the number of times a person may marry as long as they are free to do so (a divorced person needs to produce the Decree Absolute) but some ministers may refuse to conduct the ceremony for second and subsequent marriages but there are no problems in a register office.

Re-marriage in the Roman Catholic faith is possible only if a previous marriage has been annulled, which can be a complicated and lengthy process.

ENGLAND AND WALES

The law of England and Wales recognises a divorced person as 'single' so long as they can produce a Decree Absolute, after which a remarriage in a register office is conducted in exactly the same way as a first marriage.

A Decree Nisi pronounces the divorce, but neither party is free to remarry until a Decree Absolute has been granted and obtained. This is obtainable on application by the successful petitioner six weeks after the Decree Nisi.

SCOTLAND

In Scotland a preliminary pronouncement does not exist. The decree is absolute (or final) from the time of divorce, leaving the divorced person free to take steps towards re-marriage if they should so desire.

BRITISH SUBJECTS MARRYING ABROAD

The law is not the same for British subjects marrying abroad. The couple should consult a member of the British Embassy, legation or consulate in the country and district where the marriage is to take place.

BRITISH SUBJECTS MARRYING FOREIGNERS

Whether at home or abroad, there is always the matter of the woman's nationality after marriage. The couple should seek the advice of the appropriate authorities.

FOREIGNERS MARRYING IN THE UNITED KINGDOM

The law is not the same for foreigners marrying in the United Kingdom. The couple should seek an interview with the clergyman or leader of the appropriate religious sect or consult a superintendent registrar's office. They should also consult their resident representative(s) in Britain to ensure that the marriage will be legally binding in their own country.

THE MERITS OF MARRIAGE

Being married gives certain rights and protection to the husband and wife in the event of separation, divorce or the death of one partner but for unmarried couples (whose relationship holds no legal validity) there is no clearly defined legislation.

PROPERTY

There is no statute law governing the division of property upon the separation of unmarried couples. They are advised therefore to consult a solicitor so that a written agreement can be drawn up that will cater for separation and make legally valid and up-to-date wills leaving property and possessions to each other if this is their wish, otherwise the estate of the partner who dies will pass to the next of kin, namely parents or other family.

In addition to making wills, it is advisable to take out an insurance policy and to put forward the dependant partner's name for pension rights in the event of death.

Inheritance tax may be avoided by making gifts during lifetime, for anything left to a cohabitee, unlike a spouse, will be liable to tax.

CHILDREN

For separated or divorced couples, the law attempts to deal with custody/access to children in a civilised and fair way. For separated unmarried couples however, there is no legislation. Couples with dependant children are therefore certainly very well advised to consider marriage.

USEFUL ADDRESSES

The following authorities provide information on re-marriage, religious and civil, mixed religion and inter-denominational weddings, and divorce.

Baptist Union, Baptist House, 129 The Broadway, Didcot, Oxon OX11 8RT. Tel: 0235 512077.

Catholic Marriage Advisory Council, Clitheroe House, 1 Blythe Mews, Blythe Road, London W14 0NW. Tel: 071-371 1341.

Church of Scotland, Department of Communication, 121 George Street, Edinburgh EH2 4YN. Tel: 031-225 5722.

Enquiry Centre General Synod of the Church of England, Church House, Great Smith Street, London SW1P 3NZ. Tel: 071-222 9011.

General Register Office for the Isle of Man, Finch Road, Douglas, Isle of Man. Tel: 0624 5212.

General Register Office for Northern Ireland, Oxford House, 49-55 Chichester Street, Belfast BT1 4HL. Tel: 0232 235211.

General Register Office for Scotland, New Register House, Edinburgh EH1 3YT. Tel: 031-334 0380.

Jewish Marriage Council, 23 Ravenshurst Avenue, London NW4 4EL. Tel: 081-203 6311.

Methodist Church Press Office, 1 Central Buildings, Westminster, London SW1H 9NH. Tel: 071- 222 8010.

Registrar General for England and Wales, OPCS, St Catherine's House, 10 Kingsway, London WC2B 6JP. Tel: 071-242 0262.

Registrar General for Guernsey, The Greffe, Royal Court House, St Peter Port, Guernsey. Tel: 0481 725 277.

Scottish Information Office, New St Andrew's House, St James' Centre, Edinburgh EH1 3TD. Tel: 031 556 8400.

Superintendent Registrar for Jersey, States' Offices, Royal Square, St Helier, Jersey. Tel: 0534 502000.

United Reformed Church, 86 Tavistock Place, London WC1H 9RT. Tel: 071-583 8701.

CHAPTER 4

Civil Ceremony

THE REGISTER OFFICE

It is not essential for a marriage to be solemnised either by a minister or in a place of worship. Only the civil law needs to be heeded and so a marriage conducted by a Superintendent Registrar is as completely lawful as any conducted through any religious body.

The law of England and Wales recognises a divorced person as single so long as they can produce a Decree Absolute and having done so, a re-marriage in a register office is conducted on exactly the same conditions as those applying to first marriage. A Superintendent Registrar is duty bound to perform a marriage ceremony for divorced persons so long as the Decree Absolute has been granted and all other legal requirements have been met.

Second weddings are generally more informal and quieter celebrations than first marriages, especially if both partners are divorced, and are more likely to be civil ceremonies.

Some couples like to keep their wedding as quiet as possible but absolute secrecy is not possible as the proposed marriage is published by an entry in the Superintendent Registrar's notice book, which is available for everyone to view, and also notices are displayed on his noticeboard.

Civil or non-sectarian ceremonies are the most popular choice for those who are re-marrying and many couples marrying for the first time decide to marry at the register office for a variety of reasons; they may not share the same religious beliefs, preferring to marry under a neutral authority; religious convictions may have no significance for them; family objections may encourage them to take this option; or one or both of them may be divorced and unable to re-marry in church.

THE CEREMONY

A civil ceremony at a register office is a simpler and much less formal affair than a church wedding lasting only a short time. It entails no religious service and all that is required is that the marriage vows are exchanged before a Superintendent Registrar and the register signed with two witnesses being present who also sign the register. The witnesses are usually the best man and the bride's father but there is no reason why they cannot be complete strangers. As with church ceremonies, the groom places the wedding ring on the bride's third finger but this has no legal significance under civil law.

The bride and groom are asked to declare that there is no lawful impediment to their marriage. Each repeats: '*I do solemnly declare that I know not of any lawful impediment why I* (name) *may not be joined in matrimony to* (name)'. The couple are advised of the solemn and binding nature of the marriage and vows are exchanged. '*I call upon these persons here present to witness that I* (name) *do take* (name) *to be my lawful wedded husband/wife*'. The symbol of the wedding ring given to the bride is common practice. The register is then signed by each of the newlyweds and those witnessing the event.

Most register offices cannot accommodate too many people so the guests are likely to be limited to the couple's immediate family and closest friends.

The ceremony takes approximately ten minutes and members of the wedding party need to arrive promptly to ensure that other bookings remain unaffected. The order in which family, relatives and friends enter and leave the register office is unimportant but the bride and groom should be allowed to travel to the reception alone. Seating or standing arrangements in the register office are very informal.

Rules for the formality or informality of reception following a register office wedding are the same as those following a church wedding.

PREPARATIONS

The Superintendent Registrar should be consulted as soon as possible as it is important to ascertain the legal formalities of residence qualification and obtain a licence.

Under a Superintendent Registrar's Certificate of Marriage, anyone legally free to marry must be married by the Superintendent Registrar not less than twenty-one days after due notice has been given and published.

Under a Superintendent Registrar's Licence, anyone who satisfies the legal requirements, may be married by the Superintendent Registrar after the expiration of one clear working day from the date of the entry of the notice.

Register offices may be booked well in advance for Saturdays and other popular times but they may not take bookings more than three months in advance.

Where the register office wedding room is large enough, as many as fifty to sixty guests can be accommodated and there may be flower arrangements to complement the bridal party. Everything is done to make the ceremony as special as possible.

There is no reason why the bride and groom should not be attended by a full wedding party, including a best man, bridesmaids, pages and ushers if this is their wish, and if the facilities of the register office allow.

SERVICE OF BLESSING

For the couple who have not been able to re-marry in church, either because of different religious convictions or because one or both has been divorced, a service of blessing may be arranged. The service is very simple, without the marriage vows or such formalities as choir, bells and hymns. The minister gives a brief address and prayers are said to bless the marriage, followed by a gospel reading.

The question of flowers in the church and music should be discussed with the minister.

ATTIRE

In the register office brides may dress traditionally but often they wear special dresses or early cocktail attire, carry a small bouquet and wear a hat instead of a veil. There is no reason why the bride should not wear full bridal regalia in a full white gown, attended by bridesmaids and pages and the groom, best man and male guests traditionally attired in morning dress. Alternatively, it can be a very simple and small affair with informal dress for everyone where the males wear dark lounge suits.

Guests at a register office wedding generally dress

smartly as they would for a church ceremony.

At a service of blessing, the question of attire for the wedding party should be discussed with the minister.

TRANSPORT

It is perfectly acceptable for the bride to arrive at the register office in special transport such as a horse-drawn carriage or a white Rolls Royce if this is her choice.

CIVIL CEREMONY

REGISTER OFFICE

Address ______________________________

______________________ Telephone ______

Superintendent Registrar ______________________

CEREMONY

Date ______________________________

Time ______________ No. of Guests ______

	NOTES	£
Certificate/Licence		
Music		
Flora		
Photographs		
Video		
Confetti		
Other		

TOTAL £ ______________________________

CHAPTER 5

Church Ceremony

It may be rare for a minister to agree to conduct a marriage ceremony in the case of a second marriage but if he does, he must have good reason for his decision. A Church of England clergyman may not refuse to perform a marriage service so long as he is sure that there are no legal or ecclesiastical objections. He must also be satisfied that the law does in fact specifically permit a marriage, as it is a criminal offence to make a knowingly false declaration.

WIDOWS AND WIDOWERS

Widows and widowers are quite free to marry in a church.

Though the ceremony is exactly the same where a bride happens to be a widow, tradition calls for less formality. However, it would be quite in order for a widow to wear a full bridal gown with a veil, to be attended by bridesmaids and to be 'given-away' by her father if this is her wish. The bride's wishes should be followed in the matter of the service, the degree of formality, the number of guests and the scale of the reception.

The marriage of a widower is much less restricted than it is for a widow. However, it is still commonly less formal than a first wedding.

DIVORCEES

The difficulties arise when the bride and groom, one or both of them divorced, want to marry in church.

While it may be permissible under civil law, the Church of England forbids the re-marriage of a divorcee during the lifetime of a previous partner and consequently, a clergyman may legally refuse to marry in church anyone whose previous partner is still living irrespective of whether the person concerned is the injured party. Also, he cannot be compelled to permit the re-marriage to take place in his church nor can he be compelled to conduct a service for anyone who has re-married under civil law.

Therefore, no marriage service can be performed in a church of the Church of England where either the bride or groom has a previous partner still living, unless the clergyman is prepared to ignore the church authorities. There are however a few Church of England ministers who are prepared to consider individual circumstances and may be prepared to perform the ceremony with the permission of their bishop, but this is the exception rather than the rule. If a minister is prepared to ignore ecclesiastical authority or manages to obtain the permission of his bishop and agrees to conduct a marriage ceremony for a divorcee, he may discourage the presence of attendants, flowers, bell-ringers and the choir.

The whole question of divorcees marrying in church is currently under consideration by the General Synod of the Church of England but still remains highly contentious. The majority of Church of England ministers share the view of the Roman Catholic faith and would not permit a bride and groom to make vows '... until death us do part' for a second time! The marriage of divorcees will therefore, almost certainly, be a civil affair conducted by a Superintendent

Registrar in a register office.

If the church ceremony is refused and the couple feel that there is something lacking without the religious element, most ministers are prepared to conduct a service of blessing after the civil marriage and this can be a satisfactory compromise solution.

It is obviously important that divorcees enquire about all the details well in advance of the proposed wedding date so that expectations are not dashed!

FREE CHURCHES

Many of the churches of Free Church denominations have been registered by a Superintendent Registrar of Marriages as buildings in which marriages may be solemnised. Ministers of the United Reformed Church, the Baptist, Methodist and other Protestant churches take advantage of their right to become registered as 'authorised' persons to conduct the service and to act as the registrar under the civil law. Those who do not possess this authority may conduct a marriage ceremony but a Superintendent Registrar, or his deputy, must be present to record the wedding, or a separate civil ceremony must be conducted by a Superintendent Registrar in his office. Wherever the marriage venue, the register must be signed by the bridal couple and witnessed by two others. The Free churches are traditionally more liberal and normally allow a divorced person, whose ex-spouse is still living, to re-marry in church, but if the couple are strangers to Methodist or Baptist Churches for example, their chances depend on convincing the minister that there are extremely sincere reasons for wanting to re-marry in church and that they are not interested only in the aesthetics of the setting!

Although Free Churches generally view a marriage as

binding for life, each minister has discretion to consider the re-marriage of a divorced person, considering each individual case in the light of its own merits. Some ministers may adamantly refuse to marry a divorced person, others will sympathise with the injured party, and others consider that everyone is entitled to another chance.

Obviously, the couple need to make very careful enquiries before completing any wedding arrangements.

THE SOCIETY OF FRIENDS

Although the Society of Friends retains its belief in the sanctity and life-long nature of marriage, Quakers may be sympathetic and understanding of divorced persons who wish to re-marry in a Friends' Meeting as long as all the circumstances are taken into account and the monthly Meeting is satisfied that the person seeking their permission is well known to them and associated with the Meeting. It may be possible for the matter to be investigated discreetly by a group of Friends so that the monthly Meeting might be advised by them without the need to broadcast all the circumstances in public.

Any decision made by the church involved is made on the merits of each case.

ROMAN CATHOLIC CHURCH

The re-marriage of a divorced person, whose ex-spouse is still living, is strictly forbidden in the Roman Catholic Church. There are however some circumstances where the previous marriage is not recognised by the Church and is therefore deemed invalid, as in the case of a civil marriage, or where the Catholic authority's Marriage Tribunal has declared a previous marriage to be null and void which can be a complicated and lengthy process. In such cases, the Roman

Catholic Church will be prepared to marry that person provided that he or she has the legal right in civil law (by being divorced by the State from their original partner). In any event, it is essential to consult the clergyman at least six months in advance.

JEWISH FAITH

A Jewish divorcée wishing to re-marry and have her second wedding recognised under Jewish law requires a Get. This is a certificate of divorce which is issued if the husband agrees to the divorce. Further information can be obtained from the Chief Rabbi via the local Rabbi or synagogue office secretary.

GIVER-AWAY

As for a first wedding, there is no obligation on anyone to 'give the bride away', though she may invite her father or some other male relative to do so. A first-time bride marrying either a widower or a divorcée may be 'given away' by her father of course and similarly the giver-away at a bride's second marriage may still be her father but it is more usual in this case for a close friend to perform this task. Indeed, the bride may be 'given away' by a son or a brother. Alternatively, the 'giving-away' ceremony may be omitted from the service altogether where the bride walks alone, or she may walk with her groom rather than meet him at the head of the aisle.

SERVICE

Order of Service

As for first marriages, the couple need to establish in advance the exact order in which the elements of the service will occur.

Vows

There is the option to repeat short phrases after the minister or to learn phrases by rote.

Wording

There may be a choice of service in which case the couple should consult with the minister about their selection and about where best to have the reading in the ceremony as this is a matter left to his discretion.

The Book of Common Prayer of 1662 involves the bride promising to obey her husband, whereas the later version of 1928 excludes reference to obedience. The Alternative Service Book of 1980 gives the bride the choice of whether or not to promise to obey and offers variations with a selection of prayers and those who wish to be unconventional are given greater scope but it can also be conducted in a very traditional manner.

The vows may be repeated after the clergyman or recited from memory.

If a service includes some special wording, personally written for the occasion, there must naturally be no reference whatsoever to a previous marriage!

The bridal procession and the giving-away ceremony are optional and there is the opportunity for the marriage to take place during a service of Holy Communion.

Readings

Lessons suitable as readings for a second marriage include:
EPISTLE TO THE EPHESIANS chapter 3 verse 14 - end.
FIRST EPISTLE OF ST JOHN chapter 4 verses 7-12.

GOSPEL OF ST JOHN chapter 14 verses 9-12.
FIRST EPISTLE TO THE CORINTHIANS chapter 13.

Music

The choice of music helps to create the desired atmosphere and should be suitable for play on the church organ.

If order of service sheets are to be printed, the music will need to be chosen before a decision is made concerning the wording.

CONFETTI

Confetti can be a source of contention with ministers who object to the litter it causes and for this reason rice, grain, flowers or wild bird food are becoming more popular and acceptable alternatives to the paper type.

PHOTOGRAPHS AND VIDEOS

The minister may be prepared to allow cameras and videos inside the church.

SERVICE OF BLESSING

Ecclesiastical authority permits a clergyman to conduct a service of blessing following a civil wedding, though this must not resemble a wedding ceremony and there are no legal formalities. A service of blessing is a simple service, usually including hymns, prayers, a bible reading and a blessing but not an exchange of vows. It can take place at any time after the civil ceremony but often the couple, their parents and a few close friends acting as best man and maid or matron of honour go to church for the blessing before joining their guests at the reception. The service of blessing can be held in a church, at a reception in the bride's home, in a hotel, a hired hall, or in a marquee if the minister is willing to officiate.

Although this service should be both private and quiet, it can be fuller and richer at the discretion of the minister and subject to the rules of the General Synod. However, it must be clearly understood that a service of blessing is not in fact a marriage service.

CHURCH ORDER OF SERVICE

BEFORE

Music

Bells

ARRIVAL OF BRIDE

Music

ENTRY OF BRIDE

Music

MINISTER'S INTRODUCTION

Hymn

CEREMONY

Hymn

PRAYERS

Hymn

SIGNING OF REGISTER

Music

LEAVING CHURCH

Music

Bells

CHURCH ARRANGEMENTS

CHURCH

Name ______________________

Address ______________________

____

Telephone ______________________

	£
Minister	
Verger	
Organist	
Choir	
Bells	

CEREMONY

Date ______________________

Time ______________________

LICENCE/CERTIFICATE OBTAINED	
FLOWERS	
PHOTOS/VIDEO	
CONFETTI	

TOTAL £ ______________________

CHAPTER 6

Finance

RESPONSIBILITY FOR PAYMENT

For a second wedding, it would normally be inappropriate to expect either set of parents to take on the responsibility for the costs. Generally, the couple pay for their own wedding especially since it is probable that their parents contributed to their first. If the bride is divorced, she and her fiancé will generally share the expense but her parents may still offer to pay and if relatives and friends offer to contribute or help, there is no reason for their generosity to be refused.

Similarly, if the bride is a widow, she and the groom will most probably share the cost of the wedding, although her parents, relatives and friends may, of course, contribute if they wish. However, if the bride is marrying for the first time, her parents usually contribute towards the cost and host the wedding and reception in the usual way.

FINANCIAL ARRANGEMENTS

Agreements and Contracts

It is always wise to obtain written agreements for supplies and services and before commitments are made, the small print of any contracts should be examined in detail.

Estimates and Quotations

Estimates provide only a general idea of final cost whereas quotations usually state fixed prices for specified goods or services and for this reason it is advisable to obtain quotations in preference to estimates.

Deposits

If suppliers demand deposits, it is important to check the procedure in the event of cancellation.

BUDGET

All weddings incur some finance and the budget list shown on the following pages may help to organise the costings.

For most weddings, the reception takes the majority of the budget. If the budget is very limited, a restaurant meal for a small number of guests could be the solution. Other cost-cutting ideas include:

- hiring only one car to take the bride to the ceremony and the couple to the reception;
- employing either a photographer or videographer and not both;
- having only seasonal flowers;
- paying for goods and services by cheque or cash if it is not possible to clear credit card balances without incurring interest charges.

BUDGET LIST

	Estimate £	*Quotation* £
ATTIRE		
Bride		
Wedding		
Honeymoon		
Maid/Matron of Honour		
Groom		
Wedding		
Honeymoon		
Best Man		
TRANSPORT		
To ceremony		
To reception		
From reception		
PHOTOS/VIDEO		
FLOWERS		
Ceremony		
Reception		
Bride		
Maid/Matron of Honour		
Groom		
Best Man		
Guests		
CEREMONY		
Fees		
RECEPTION		

Deposit	*Paid*	*Balance*	*Paid*	**TOTAL**
£	✓	£	✓	**£**

BUDGET LIST *continued*

	Estimate £	*Quotation* £
HONEYMOON		
Holiday		
Insurance		
Spending		
Passports/Visas		
Inoculations		
STATIONERY		
Invitations		
Order of Service Sheets		
Menus		
Thank-yous		
Keepsake Album		
GIFTS		
To Groom ring		
To Bride ring		
To Maid/Matron of Honour		
To Best Man		
PRE-WEDDING PARTIES		
Hen		
Stag		
Others		
SPECIAL SERVICES		
TOTAL £		

Deposit	*Paid*	*Balance*	*Paid*	**TOTAL**
£	✓	£	✓	**£**

CHAPTER 7

Reception

Although ceremonies for second weddings tend to be comparatively simple and informal, there is no reason to restrict the reception afterwards; the traditional wedding breakfast, wedding cake, floral decorations, toasts and speeches are all perfectly acceptable.

Feasts are a natural way of celebrating many occasions and second marriages are no exceptions but on the other hand there is absolutely no necessity to provide a meal and entertainment if this is the couple's wish. After all, the whole purpose of a reception after any wedding is to allow the guests to congratulate the newlyweds, join in the toasts to the health and happiness of the couple, witness the cutting of the cake and to wish them well as they leave for their honeymoon. The meal itself is incidental to the celebrations and is served because guests will probably be hungry long before the couple leave for honeymoon.

Having said this, most receptions do include the provision of food for which the catering is a vital consideration and choosing the right time, atmosphere, theme and venue helps to ensure the success of the celebrations.

SETTING

Hotels

Although probably the most expensive option, hotels are able to provide maximum facilities including overnight accommodation.

When considering more than one venue, it may be advisable to sample the food by having a meal at the prospective hotel prior to booking. When the venue is selected, a firm booking should be made and written confirmation obtained.

Home

Home receptions often have an intimate, comfortable and personal atmosphere. Although they offer maximum freedom and flexible timing, numbers will inevitably be limited and organisation requires plenty of detail.

Other ideas include a marquee garden party but the time of year and weather elements are always a risk.

FOOD

Meal type options include sit-down hot or cold (fork buffet) and stand-up finger buffet.

Food need not be extravagant or exotic, but should be delicious, attractive and practical. A selection of well chosen dishes to suit various tastes and served attractively will be much enjoyed.

A sit-down meal provides the opportunity to serve hot dishes such as soups and desserts. If guests are to stand, a finger buffet is advisable.

For very good reasons, guests may have special dietary requirements and these will need to be planned in advance.

CATERERS

Outside Caterer

Apart from the obvious advantage of having things done by someone else and carried out professionally, caterers are able to suggest suitable menus and provide all the necessary! Standards and prices do vary so it is therefore advisable to compare their services and terms carefully.

Self-caterer

The considerable effort necessary to self-cater needs very careful consideration.

Cocktails and hors-d'oeuvres could be served in the afternoon as an alternative to a sit-down luncheon or dinner. A small dinner party for six to eight guests would perhaps be manageable.

CAKE

The cake stands in the centre of the top table at a sit-down reception and in the centre of the food table at a buffet.

Cake-makers

A traditional wedding cake should be made at least four months in advance of the wedding.

DRINK

Guests will, of course, want liquid refreshments. If supplying drinks, quantities will naturally depend on the number and thirst of the guests and a reasonable range should be provided, including a plentiful supply of mixers, fresh fruit juices, soft drinks and non-alcoholic wines.

Arrival at the Reception

As an alternative to the traditional sherry, red and white wine may be served.

Accompaniment to the Meal

The tradition of white wine with fish and red with most meats may no longer seem appropriate, particularly since most people prefer white.

The Toasts

There is a wide range of champagne to suit various budgets. Less expensive alternatives to champagne, include sparkling white or rosé wines.

After the Meal

Although very formal meals are sometimes followed by dessert wine, brandy, port or liqueurs, it is acceptable to serve tea and coffee and if there is a bar, guests may pay for their own drinks or a sum of money may be allocated so that they start paying when this is exhausted.

RECEIVING LINE

At an informal reception it is not necessary to have a traditional receiving line. The bride and groom may simply greet guests together at the door and let them mingle freely. If the greeting of guests is dispensed with entirely, the bride and groom must be sure to thank each guest before the reception comes to a close. Where there is to be a receiving line, the hostess and host are usually first. Divorced parents should not be expected to stand together if this is likely to cause problems. New partners are not normally included but personal circumstances will dictate the most appropriate line-up. Common sense and an awareness of other people's feelings must prevail when planning the details.

GUEST BOOK

Although it is not necessary to have a guest book at the reception, its supervision is a pleasurable activity which may be assigned to a child of the newlyweds. Located near the receiving line, the child reminds each guest to sign.

SEATING

A stand-up buffet type reception demands no formal seating arrangements except to say that guests can only be expected to stand for a short time. Seats should be provided for the elderly and an area set aside for young children.

For a more formally seated reception, the top table may be reserved for the wedding party. However, special circumstances such as divorce, will obviously need to be handled tactfully. If possible, children of the bride and groom from previous marriage should be seated at the top table whether or not they have played a part in the earlier proceedings. Divorced parents and their ex-spouses should not be seated together unless they are on particularly friendly terms and this arrangement causes no ill-feeling amongst other guests.

An alternative to traditional seating arrangements is a room full of round tables which can provide a much more relaxed atmosphere where guests are grouped tactfully with a good mix of men and women.

ENTERTAINMENT

Music adds to the enjoyment of many occasions. The size and formality of the reception will determine the type of music which can be anything from a live band to a tape recording.

Although personal preference will prevail, variety

keeps most people happy especially where the guests' ages may range from one to seventy. For the quieter reception, sophisticated background music may be a good choice.

For the children's entertainment, a clown or magician could keep them interested for hours. Videos are also another idea and are particularly useful for keeping the younger guests fully occupied throughout the reception.

CHAPTER 8

Honeymoon

There is the tendency for couples marrying for the second time to forgo a honeymoon, dismissing it as an unnecessary expense but if at all possible a break away from the pressures of home is recommended. It will be a good time to confirm the new relationship together and to make the wedding even more of an occasion to remember.
With holidays being booked nearly six months in advance these days, honeymoon reservations need early consideration and attention especially if travelling in high season and to a popular holiday resort.

If the wedding precedes the Summer vacation, then a longer main holiday my be possible but if a holiday is planned for later in the year it may be preferable to have a short honeymoon break immediately following the wedding.

It is advisable to choose a holiday that suits both partners such as one based on shared interests but if the prospective groom arranges a surprise, the prospective bride should be given an indication of climate and activities.

Many hotels in Britain offer a free bedroom if there has been a sizeable reception held in the hotel. In addition, there are hotels and guest houses which offer budget honeymoon deals with four-poster beds, champagne and free gifts laid on.

CHAPTER 9

Duties

ATTENDANTS

Attendants at a second marriage tend to be restricted to a maid or matron of honour (depending on whether the woman friend is single or married) and a best man.

Older children from previous marriage may serve in such roles or as bridesmaids and ushers if desired. A widow remarrying might want to give a responsible role to a grown-up or teenage son, for example the duties of best man if the groom agrees. However, it should be borne in mind that not all young men would feel at ease with the situation and might prefer the role of usher. Flower girls and ring bearers are usually between three and seven years old whereas junior bridesmaids and ushers are between eight and fourteen. The bride and groom may wish to walk the aisle alone but it is quite acceptable for the bride's father or a son to have this honour.

Owing to the increase in the number of remarriages, more children than ever before are acquiring one or two step-parents and, in many cases, step-brothers and step-sisters. Children have for a long time been included in both first and second marriage ceremonies as flower girls, ring bearers and junior bridesmaids, and in the case of second weddings, it is essential that children from previous marriage are part of the proceedings so that they do not feel excluded from the occasion in any way. It is obviously important to include all children and not just some! After all, it is not their choice to become step-children! Alternatively, if there are to be no attendants and the marriage is to take place in church, children may read a special verse or lesson if the minister agrees. It is also important to allocate special duties to children so that they feel important throughout the reception. They could be asked to greet the guests, supervise the guest book, or form part of the receiving line even if they are not members of the wedding party.

If there are children from previous marriage, then obviously the couple will have spent time beforehand getting them used to the idea of the marriage and the new arrangements which will follow. Being a step-parent can be a difficult role and it is important to try to establish a good relationship with the children as early as possible and enlist the partner's help and support.

As soon as the wedding date is set, the bride should ask those whom she would like to have serve as her attendants and if they would be willing to do so. They can be asked in person, by telephone or by letter. The feelings of a former spouse must be considered at the planning stage and it is wise to discuss ideas before suggestions are made to the children.

THE WEDDING PARTY WHO'S WHO

Name	*Address*	*Telephone*
Bride		
Groom		
Maid/Matron of Honour		
Best Man		
Others		

BRIDE'S AND GROOM'S DIARY

PREPARATIONS

Hold discussions

Announce news

Appoint attendants

Hold engagement party

Compile guest list

Compile budget

Book ceremony

Book reception and entertainment

Order cake

Book photographer/videographer

Book transport

Acquire attire

Book florist

Order stationery

Plan and book honeymoon

Arrange passports, traveller's cheques and inoculations

Acquire rings and gifts for attendants

Send invitations

Obtain licence

Write speech (groom)

Hold rehearsal, hen and stag parties

Confirm arrangements with all service suppliers

Write thank-you letters for gifts received

Remove 'first' wedding ring

THE DAY

AFTER THE HONEYMOON

Order photographs

Deal with documentation

MAID/MATRON ON HONOUR

A maid of honour is an unmarried lady attendant. A matron of honour is a married lady attendant. It is possible to have both a maid and a matron of honour in which case it is the maid of honour who takes precedence, holding the bride's bouquet and serving as a witness. However, it is more usual to have either one or the other rather than both. As for a first wedding, there is no absolute need for the bride to be surrounded by bridesmaids. The bride may prefer to have only one assistant, perhaps a married sister or close married friend, particularly if the bride is older.

A maid or matron of honour acts as adviser, messenger and general assistant to the bride. Her duties are those of a chief bridesmaid in that she assists the bride as much as possible with the wedding planning and preparations, attending the hen night and on the day ensuring that the bride looks her best. She is the bride's consultant, relieving her of as many chores as possible especially on the wedding day when she will be near to the bride throughout the proceedings and is the equivalent of the groom's best man.

DIARY

PREPARATIONS

Buy gift for bride

Acquire attire

Help bride with arrangements and preparations

Attend hen night

THE DAY

- Assist the bride throughout the day
- Help bride to arrange her gown
- Form part of the bridal procession
- If there is no procession before the service wait for the bride at the chancel steps
- Relieve the bride of her bouquet
- Sign register if called upon to do so
- Form part of the receiving line
- Help bride to change

BEST MAN

The groom's assistant will be his closest friend, chosen for his qualities of common sense and responsibility.

As for first marriages, his major role is to ensure that the groom gets to the ceremony on time. As there is usually less formality at a bride's second marriage and as it is more likely to be held before a registrar rather than in church, there are fewer demands on the best man.

It is a great honour to be asked to be best man, a vote of the groom's friendship and confidence but the groom must remember that the job should give his friend pleasure and that it is not everyone who relishes the responsibility!

Ushers may be recruited but as the ceremony is usually less formal, there is rarely need for them at a bride's second marriage.

BEST MAN'S FACT FILE

THE WEDDING PARTY WHO'S WHO

Name	*Address*	*Telephone*
Bride		
Groom		
Maid/Matron of Honour		
Others		

DETAILS

Wedding Date

Ceremony

Venue

Arrival Time

Officiant

BEST MAN'S FACT FILE

DETAILS *continued*

Telephone

Fees - when payable

Confetti rules

Photo/video restrictions

Parking arrangements

Attire

Hire Firm

Address

Telephone

Fitting Dates

Collection Date

Return Date

Flora

Stag Night

Date

Time

Transport

Photographer

Name

Telephone

Reception

Venue

Contact

Telephone

Time

BEST MAN'S FACT FILE

DETAILS *continued*

Parking facilities

Number of guests

Toastmaster

Meal commences at

Speeches commence at

People to thank

Bar facilities

Entertainment

Leaving time

Transport

To church

To reception

To honeymoon

Car hire/taxi

Firm

Address

Telephone

Cars to be supplied

Collection/delivery time

Return time

BEST MAN'S DIARY

PREPARATIONS

Purchase wedding gift

Assist groom in preparations

Arrange and acquire attire

Organise stag night

Arrange transport

Prepare and practise speech

Check parking arrangements

Purchase a spare ring

Ensure groom's safety on and after stag night

Collect order of service sheets

THE DAY

Ensure that the groom is properly dressed

Accompany groom to church in plenty of time

Pay church fees

Pose for photographs

Take seat in front pew on the right

Take charge of groom's hat and gloves

Wait on the right side of and a little behind the groom at the ceremony

Move forward with groom to stand in front of the steps

Hand over the ring/s

Escort maid/matron of honour to vestry

Sign register if called upon to do so

Escort maid/matron of honour out of the church following the bride and groom

Pose for photographs

BEST MAN'S DIARY

THE DAY *continued*

Leave for the reception with the maid/matron of honour after bride and groom

Join receiving line if required to do so

Mingle with guests

Make speech, propose toast and read any messages

Ensure that going-away attire is ready

Help groom to change

Deal with transport and luggage for the bride's and groom's departure

GIVER-AWAY

Although it is traditional for the father of the bride, or in his absence an older male relative or close friend, to accompany his daughter down the aisle and 'give her away', it is perfectly acceptable for the bride to walk alone, to have her children or another relative escort her.

GIVER-AWAY DIARY

PREPARATIONS

Acquire attire

Write speech

THE DAY

Escort the bride to church

Arrive last with bride

Lead procession to chancel steps with the bride on right arm

Take bride's right hand and give to the minister at the appropriate time

Give away the bride

GIVER-AWAY DIARY

THE DAY *continued*

Proceed to vestry followed by the best man and the maid/matron of honour

Leave church after bride, groom, best man and maid/matron of honour

Pose for photographs

Leave for reception after the bride, groom, best man and maid/matron of honour

Propose the toast to the bride and groom when called upon by the best man

SPEECHES AND TOASTS

Speeches at all weddings include the toasts and usually occur after the meal followed by the cutting of the cake.

A second marriage is a celebration that calls for toasts and there is no difference in content between those proposed at a first wedding and those proposed at a second.

However, the speeches at a woman's second marriage are subtly different from those at first weddings; they will probably not have the same lightness and gaiety as the tone needs to be a little more serious. As for any wedding, the guests simply expect a few sincere words, they do not want lengthy oratories. Following each toast, the guests stand, raise their glasses, repeat the toast and drink to whoever is mentioned.

Order of Toasts

Each speaker is announced briefly by the toastmaster or, in his absence, the best man who frequently performs this role.

First Toast

The giver-away, who is normally a male friend, stands and says a few words about the bride and groom before proposing the toast to the health and happiness of the bride and groom. The toast may still be proposed by the bride's father, but this is fairly unusual; he is not, after all, giving away his daughter in marriage this time! The toast would normally be proposed by a male friend.

Reply

The groom responds on behalf of the bride and himself.

Second Toast

The groom proposes a toast to the maid or matron of honour.

Reply

The best man replies on behalf of the maid or matron of honour and bridesmaids, and reads any congratulatory telemessages and other messages as he would at a first wedding.

Typical First Speech and Toast

'Ladies and Gentlemen,

It's a real pleasure for me to propose the health and happiness of Nel and Sam. They are both good friends of mine and when I learned that they were to join their lives together, I couldn't have been happier. I think all of us in this room must feel the same. They are so eminently suited, if I may use a rather old-fashioned term. I am, in any case, a rather old-fashioned person and the sight of a good marriage puts happiness in my heart.

Let us raise our glasses then to two of the nicest people I know, or perhaps I might now say, one of the nicest couples I know.'

Typical Groom's Response to First Toast

'Ladies and gentlemen,

It was most kind of you to say such nice things about Nel - my wife as I must learn to call her - and myself. We're both touched by the knowledge that we have so many good friends who have come here today to wish us well. We hope to welcome all of you in our new home when we have settled down.

I would like to express my special gratitude to Nancy, who helped Nel so much with the wedding arrangements and to Simon who sorted out one or two tangles for me.

On behalf of my wife and myself then, thank you.'

Planning

A speech read from notes is disastrous and if reciting purely from memory this may also present problems. The best method is to refer to brief 'headline' note cards which serve as memory-joggers so that the main points are not forgotten. This method gives a speech shape and allows some flexibility for improvisation.

It goes without explanation that speeches at a second marriage must be very carefully worded and no mention made of sensitive topics such as a previous marriage or phrases such as 'second time around'.

Appropriate quotations used sensitively can be quite useful in a speech.

The use of a tape recorder and a mirror, or a video recorder, can be very enlightening when practising a speech. Little idiocyncracies such as restless hands and shuffling feet, quickly become apparent and can be corrected making a much more confident performance.

DRAFT SPEECH

CHAPTER 10

Guest List

For a second marriage where the bride and groom are hostess and host, they will compile the guest list themselves.

A divorced partner may be in a dilemma concerning good friends from a previous marriage, but then they always have the option to refuse the invitation if they feel that their presence would be inappropriate. It is obviously insensitive to invite a former spouse unless the relationship is still very good. However, children from a previous marriage should be invited and if they are expected to perform the roles of attendants, the agreement of the former partner should be sought and given.

In the case of a widow or widower who remains close to the family of the late partner, it may be appropriate to invite them to the wedding providing that this will not create any ill-feeling. Of course, they may choose not to attend but should not be offended by receiving an invitation. It would be especially appropriate to invite them if there are children from the previous marriage since this indicates the continuance of their relationship with their grandchildren.

The guest list should therefore include:

Family of both the bride and groom.
The couple's mutual friends and those who may have been close to either partner during previous marriage and have remained so.
Former in-laws if still close and if their presence will not cause any uncomfortable feelings.

GUEST LIST

TOTAL NUMBERS		Invited:	Accepted:
	Adults		
	Children		

Name	*Address*

Individual needs such as special dietary requirements and wheelchair access should be considered at the planning stage.

Telephone	*Invited* ✓	*Reply* ✓	✕	*Special Needs, eg dietary requirements*

CHAPTER 11

Announcements and Printing

PRESS ANNOUNCEMENTS

An announcement for a second marriage is the same as for a first in that it follows the same form as the invitation except that it announces rather than invites and the bride's name may be different from that of her parents if they issue the announcement. The announcement need not be issued by the bride's parents, it can be issued by the bride and groom or by both the bride's and groom's parents together. An older couple's announcement would normally exclude mention of parents or grandparents and would instead elaborate on the ceremony, professions and future plans. There is no requirement to state whether it is a first or second marriage.

Some couples prefer a quiet and private ceremony and simply invite their very closest relations and friends to the ceremony or may even choose to marry in front of only two independent witnesses such as the register office clerks. The couple may then decide to announce the news by way of notes, handwritten or printed, to relations and friends after, instead of before, the event.

If a formerly married pair are no longer on friendly terms and the re-marriage to someone else would be threatened by disruption if the date were made public, then the best policy is to keep the date a secret, even from the children of the previous marriage until the wedding is imminent. The former spouse may be told of the marriage after the event and informed that the children had no prior knowledge.

Announcements place no obligation on a reader to send a gift, although they may chose to do so.

A couple of examples of announcements issued by the couple:

WHEN THE WOMAN WAS PREVIOUSLY WIDOWED

The bride uses her former husband's name.

Mrs Sam South
and
Mr William West
announce their marriage
....

WHEN THE WOMAN WAS PREVIOUSLY DIVORCED

The bride uses her own first name.

Mrs Nel South
and
Mr William West
announce their marriage
....

An alternative is not to include titles at all but to use only first names.

Following a Service of Blessing

A Service of Blessing
was held yesterday/on...
at St Mark's Church, Northton
after the marriage of
Mrs Nel Smith
to/and
Mr William West
The Rev G Green officiated

Or, briefly

The marriage took place quietly
in Northton
on 2 May 19..
between
Mrs Nel Smith
and
Mr William West

INFORMAL INVITATIONS

If the wedding is small or if there is little advance notice, a personal letter, handwritten card or telephone call is both sufficient and acceptable. Although facsimile (fax) machines are a most efficient means of communicating on paper, they are still used primarily for business purposes and consequently should not be used for personal exchanges such as for wedding invitations.

Suggested wording for a letter:

Dear Jenny and Alan

Ned and I are to be married at St. Mark's Church, Northton/Northton Register Officer on Saturday 2 May 19..

We hope that you both will come to the church/register office, and afterwards to the reception at Stone Manor, Northton.

With much love from both of us.
Nel

Suggested wording for a card:

Nel North and Sam South
invite you
to celebrate their
marriage
on Saturday 2 May 19..
at St Mark's Church/
Northton Register Office
Northton

RSVP

Invitations to an informal wedding should be sent out three weeks before the wedding.

FORMAL INVITATIONS

Invitations are not normally sent out by the bride's mother but by a friend of the bride. However, if the bride's parents are in fact hosting the occasion, then they would send out the invitations or they can be sent by the bride and groom. The bride may wish to invite only close family to a register office, and then invite additional guests to a reception afterwards.

For a formal wedding, engraved or thermographed invitations may be sent. Invitations should be ordered as soon as the date and times of the ceremony and reception have been confirmed. Engraved or thermographed work may take a couple of months to process and this needs to be borne in mind when considering that invitations should be despatched to guests four to six weeks before a formal reception.

Style

The style of invitations should reflect the formality and style of the wedding. There are numerous styles from which to choose about which stationers and printers can advise.

Wording

The bride's surname is not normally included on the invitations. The wording for the formal invitations would be similar to that for first marriages and again may be handwritten, pre-printed or specially printed. When the couple are hosting the occasion, the invitations should reflect this fact in the wording.

It is useful for guests to know the type of reception so that they may plan suitable dress and meal arrangements for the day. The inclusion of the words 'dinner or luncheon or buffet reception' on the invitations is acceptable.

Examples:

WEDDING GIVEN BY BRIDE'S PARENTS

Mr and Mrs N/Ned North
request the pleasure of your company/
request the company of ...
at the marriage/wedding of
their daughter
Nel South
to
Mr William West
at St Mark's Church/Northton Register Office
Northton
on Saturday 2 May 19..
at 2.30 pm
and at the reception afterwards
at Stone Manor, Northton

RSVP
(Address)

For a widow re-marrying in church, her parents may issue the invitations just as they would for a daughter who is single, though they would use her married name:

Mrs Nel South

Wedding given by Groom's Parents

Mr and Mrs Wilfred West
request the honour of your presence
at the marriage of
Mrs N/Nel South
to their son
William West
....

Wedding given by Single Parent

Mrs/Mr Nancy/Ned North
requests the honour of your presence
at the marriage of
her/his daughter
Nel South
....

Wedding given by Widowed or Divorced Mother, Recently Remarried

Mr and Mrs Edward East
request the honour of your presence
at the marriage of
her daughter
Mrs Nel South
.....

WEDDING GIVEN BY BOTH PARENTS WHO ARE DIVORCED AND REMARRIED

> *Mr and Mrs Edward East*
> *and*
> *Mr and Mrs Ned North*
> *request the honour of your presence*
> *at the marriage of*
> *Nel South*
> *to William West*
> ....

When both of the bride's parents are sharing expenses equally, the bride's mother's name precedes the father's and she acts as hostess at the reception but if the father is solely responsible for providing the finance, his name should appear first.

WEDDING GIVEN BY BRIDE AND GROOM

For a wedding hosted by the bride and groom, the invitations can be either formal or informal. Although a wedding may be given by the bride and groom, they may still send out the invitations in the parents' name. The bride may send out the invitations in her own name:

> *Mrs Nel South and Mr William West*
> *request the pleasure of your company/*
> *request the company of ...*
> *at our marriage*
> *at St Mark's Church/Northton Register Office*
> *Northton*
> *on Saturday 2 May 19.. at 2.30 pm*
> *and at the reception afterwards*
> *Stone Manor, Northton*

Or

The pleasure of your company
is requested
at the marriage of
Nel South
to William West
on ...
at ...
at ...

Or

Mrs Nel South
and
Mr William West
request the honour of your presence
at their marriage
on ...
at ...
at...

Or

Nel South
and
William West
invite you to share in the joy
of the beginning of a new life together
when they exchange vows of marriage
on ...
at ...
at ...

Or

Our joy will be more complete
if you can share in the ceremony
of our marriage
on ...
at ...
at...
and celebrate with us
during the reception following
at ...

NEL SOUTH AND WILLIAM WEST

Invitations may be worded to include children:

Nel South
and
William West
together with their children
request the pleasure of your company/
request the company of

....

at their marriage/wedding
at St Mark's Church,
Northton
on Saturday 2 May 19..
at 4.00 pm
and at the reception afterwards
at Stone Manor,
Northton

Or

Natalie and Nathan South
and
Winnie and Wally West
request the pleasure of your company/
request the company of
....

at the marriage/wedding of
their parents
Nel South
and
William West
at St Mark's Church, Northton
on Saturday 2 May 19.. at 4.00 p.m.
and at the reception afterwards
at Stone Manor, Northton

WEDDING GIVEN BY SON OR DAUGHTER

Mr/Mrs/Miss Nathan/Natalie South
request the honour of your presence
at the marriage of
his/her/their mother
Mrs Nel South
to
Mr William West
....

Reception Only

The pleasure of your company
is requested
at the wedding reception
of
Nel South
and
William West
. . . .

Service of Blessing

For a service of blessing after a civil marriage, it may be a private service held between the register office ceremony and the reception, but sometimes it is possible to invite guests to the blessing and then to the reception:

Nel North
and
William West
invite
. . . .

to the blessing of their marriage
at
St Mark's Church
Northton
. . . .

Or

> *Mr and Mrs Ned North*
> *request the pleasure of your company*
> *at a Service of Blessing*
> *following the marriage*
> *of their daughter*
> *Nel South*
> *to*
> *Mr William West*
> *at St Mark's Church*
> *Northton*
> *on Saturday 2 May 19..*
> *at 3.00 pm*
> *and afterwards at*
> *Stone Manor*
> *Northton*
>
> RSVP
> (Address)

There are many variations on the traditional formal wording and sample books of invitations provide many ideas to suit most circumstances.

INVITATIONS - WORDING

ORDER OF SERVICE SHEETS

Pre-printed order of service sheets enable the congregation to follow the service and hymns without referring back and forth from prayer book to hymn book. The minister needs to advise prior to the placing of the printing order.

MENUS

If there is a choice of fare, menu cards may be printed for the guests' convenience.

OTHER STATIONERY AND SOUVENIRS

Many items such as napkins, napkin rings, drink mats, etc. may be monogrammed and kept as souvenirs.

THANK-YOU CARDS AND LETTERS

Thank-you cards and letters may be pre-printed with new name and address and sent to guests who have sent gifts or helped towards the day.

ORDER of SERVICE
MENU
Invitation

PRINTING REQUIREMENTS

	Invitations	*Order of Service Sheets*
Supplier		
Address		
Telephone		
Fax		
Number required		
Style		
Size		
Paper/Card		
Paper/Card Colour		
Print:		
Style		
Colour		

Thank-yous (letterheadings)	*Other*

CHAPTER 12

Photography and Videography

An appointment with the photographer and/or videographer should be made as soon as possible after the wedding date is confirmed at which the schedule for the day should be discussed.

PHOTOGRAPHER

Most photographers offer wedding packages but these do vary. Many charge a standard fee which includes attendance at the wedding to take a certain number of photographs and insist on a deposit at the time of booking.

After the wedding, the photographer will print proofs of all the shots from which the bride and groom may make their choices.

VIDEOGRAPHER

With the advancement of technological achievements and creative editing, professional videographers can now promise to produce tapes of exceptional quality.

Deciding on the right videographer involves research and as with many services, the best way to find a reliable one is through the recommendations of family or friends. The wedding photographer may be able to suggest a videographer with whom he has a good working relationship. It is only the professionals who have the appropriate equipment and skills to do the job correctly and it is worth taking the time and effort to find a reputable person. He should use only broadcast quality industrial cameras for the clearest and sharpest results. If a videographer shoots the wedding and then hands over the tape at the end of the day instead of doing the post production work, then he has not done his job! When viewing samples of their work, it is wise to look for smooth transitions, clear sound, proper lighting and sharp images.

Costs are based on the amount of editing done, the number and types of cameras used, the length of the wedding and special effects. Still photographs, names, titles and music all add polish to the final film, although too many effects can overdo the production making it look amateurish. Some packages include a one, one and a half or two hour finished tape whereas others are more condensed and easier to view lasting for forty-five minutes. Highlight tapes are increasing in popularity as an addition to video packages.

Permission is needed for the taking of photographs or the making of videos in religious establishments. Some ministers feel that such recordings of the ceremony interfere with the religious atmosphere. The photographer or videographer will need to be informed of the restrictions. If the ceremony situation is inconvenient for the photography session or filming, the reception venue may provide a more attractive setting.

Amateur photographers or videographers who agree to oblige, should be re-imbursed the cost of the film regardless of the results!

PHOTOGRAPHER - VIDEOGRAPHER

Photographer/Videographer

Address

Telephone

Fax

Package details

Price increases

Deposit

Cancellation policy

Confirmation in writing

Proofs:

Ready date

Return date

Photos:

Ready date

TOTAL £

THE PHOTOGRAPHS/VIDEO

The officiant will confirm whether or not photography or videography is allowed. He may not allow the service itself to be photographed or videod but may perr it *some* recording to take place.

PHOTOGRAPHS/VIDEO

Wedding Date

	Time	*Type of Shots*
Before Ceremony		
Location		
At Ceremony		
Location		
During Ceremony		
After Ceremony		
Formal After Ceremony		
Location		
At Reception		
Location		
Special Requests		

CHAPTER 13

Attire

BRIDE

It is true to say that for a bride who is divorced, widowed or marrying late whether marrying in church or in a register office, her dress is often simpler in style and more restrained than the traditional regalia. A second-time bride would not normally wear a veil for instance and though it is usual for women to wear some form of headdress in church, this is not obligatory in the Church of England, the Roman Catholic Church and some of the Free Churches.

There are some people who firmly believe that a second-time bride should not wear a full traditional white gown and veil because they are symbols of virginity and innocence traditionally reserved for maidenhood. On the other hand, there are those who believe that every bride has every right to look like a bride and that to choose white or ivory, long or short, with or without the veil is a valid fashion choice depending on the formality of the wedding.

A civil marriage in a register office can be as informal or as dressy as the parties concerned wish. Weddings can be conducted in full bridal regalia with attendants and the groom, best man and male guests in morning dress; in fact everything to make the ceremony as special as possible. Alternatively, it can be a very simple and small affair with everyone dressed informally. For the first-time bride marrying in a register office, she may wear a full white bridal gown and veil if this is her choice, and be attended by bridesmaids, and given-away by her father of course.

Though the ceremony is exactly the same where a bride happens to be a widow, tradition calls for less formality and this is also reflected in her dress and suggests the omission of a full white wedding gown and veil but this traditional approach would be totally appropriate if she is marrying for the first time and it is the groom who is widowed.

Women over the age of forty generally look better in attire other than wedding gowns, such as formal evening wear, dressy suits or dinner/cocktail outfits and although any of these choices may be pure white, off-white or pastel shades tend to be the most flattering. Some brides choose to marry in an outfit which can be worn again at social events but choose something rather special. A well-cut suit or long silk dress would be suitable, usually in pastel colours with a corsage or small simple bouquet and a hat or a headdress of flowers to replace the veil.

ATTENDANTS AND MOTHERS

The guidelines for correct attire applying to first weddings, are appropriate for attendants and mothers at second weddings whether daytime or evening, informal or formal.

ATTIRE
BRIDE AND MAID/MATRON OF HONOUR

	Bride
WEDDING	
Supplier	
Address	
Telephone	
Fax	
Collection date	
Return date if hired	
Payment details	
Cancellation policy	
	£
Dress	
Headdress	
Footwear	
Underwear	
Accessories	
Jewellery	
Make-up	
Perfume	
HONEYMOON	
Outfit	
Accessories	
Payment details	
TOTAL £	

Maid/Matron of Honour	*Bridesmaids*
£	£

ATTIRE
BRIDE AND MAID/MATRON OF HONOUR

IDEAS

GROOM AND BEST MAN

There is no reason to suggest that the groom and the best man should not wear formal attire (morning dress) or if they prefer something less formal - lounge suits. However, though the ceremony is exactly the same where a bride happens to be a widow, tradition calls for less formality and suggests that the groom should wear a dark lounge suit rather than the formal attire usual for a bride's first wedding.

Traditional morning dress is usually a black or grey three-piece with a tail coat together with a top hat and gloves. It is more usual to hire morning dress owing to the high expense of purchase.

At a formal evening reception, the groom wears a bow tie; for day time his choices can vary from formal wear to a blazer and slacks.

Whatever degree of formality the groom decides upon, the best man and the rest of the male members of the wedding party should follow. It is the groom's buttonhole which distinguishes him from other members.

ATTIRE
GROOM AND BEST MAN

	Groom
WEDDING	
Supplier	
Address	
Telephone	
Collection date	
Return date if hired	
Payment details	
Collection policy	
	£
Jacket	
Trousers	
Waistcoat	
Shirt	
Top Hat	
Shoes	
Socks	
Underwear	
Accessories	
HONEYMOON	
Outfit	
Accessories	
Payment details	
TOTAL £	

Best Man

£

CHAPTER 14

Transport

As for first weddings, there are no specific rules concerning the responsibility for transport except that everyone must be transported safely, no one should be left behind and that the best man gets the groom to the ceremony venue in plenty of time.

At a register office, it is important that members of the wedding party are assembled promptly at the pre-determined time so that other bookings remain unaffected. It is acceptable for the bride and groom to arrive together and they should be allowed to travel to the reception alone.

The choice of transport is therefore a matter of personal choice but using a hire or taxi firm does have advantages in that everyone has the opportunity to enjoy themselves fully without having to worry about driving.

Regardless of arrangements, it is sensible to have a few reserve cars on stand-by in case of emergencies.

If the style of the day is a simple register office affair, the wedding party may simply arrange to meet at the venue or the bride might travel with one of the witnesses and the groom with the other.

TRANSPORT

VENUES:

Ceremony ____________________

Reception ____________________

TRANSPORT

Booked ____________________

Supplier ____________________

Address ____________________

Telephone

Emergency ____________________

Supplier ____________________

Address ____________________

Telephone

TRANSPORT

	Notes
TO CHURCH	
Bride	
Giver-away	
Maid/Matron of Honour	
Other attendants	
Groom & Best Man	
TO RECEPTION	
Bride & Groom	
Best Man	
Maid/Matron of Honour	
Other attendants	
FROM RECEPTION	
Bride & Groom	
Best Man	
Maid/Matron of Honour	
Other attendants	

TOTAL £

Notes

CHAPTER 15

Rings and Gifts for the Wedding Party

RINGS

A woman who plans to re-marry following her divorce should not wear her new engagement ring until the divorce is final. Any woman who has been wearing an engagement ring from her previous marriage, should remove it and not wear it again when she becomes re-engaged. The former ring could be passed onto a son so that he may use it some day as an engagement ring for his future bride or the stones may be reset and used as another form of jewellery for the bride or for a daughter. A wedding ring from a previous marriage may be worn until the day of the second wedding at which time it should be removed and not worn again.

Although it is legal to be married without a ring or to borrow one for the ceremony, it is more usual to have a new ring for the wedding.

The choice of rings available continues to be more and

more extensive and it is obviously worth considering more than one option.

Instead of diamonds, couples often decide on less expensive stones for engagement rings. Birthstones (or Month stones) are popular and are generally accepted as follows:-

January	Garnet	*Constancy*
February	Amethyst	*Sincerity*
March	Bloodstone	*Courage*
April	Diamond	*Innocence/Lasting Love*
May	Emerald	*Success/Hope*
June	Pearl	*Purity/Health*
July	Ruby	*Love/Contentment*
August	Sardonyx	*Married Bliss*
September	Sapphire	*Wisdom/Repentance*
October	Opal	*Hope*
November	Topaz	*Fidelity/Cheerfulness*
December	Turquoise	*Harmony*

The majority of wedding rings sold are 9 carat gold which best withstand the friction of two rings rubbing together over the years.

GIFTS FOR EACH OTHER AND THE WEDDING PARTY

Gifts for the wedding party members show appreciation for their contribution to and participation at the wedding. Popular gifts include jewellery, compacts, goblets and china.

RINGS & GIFTS FOR THE WEDDING PARTY

	Bride
Supplier	
Address	
Telephone	
Ring/Gift	
Ring Size	
Engravings	
Alterations	
Collection date	
Policy	
Exchange	
Return	
Refund	
Repair	
Replacement	
Guarantee	
Insurance	
Payment dates	
TOTAL £	

Groom	Maid/Matron of Honour	Best Man

CHAPTER 16

Flowers

Flowers complete and complement the ladies attire and provide displays both at the ceremony and at the reception.

BOUQUETS

A bride's bouquet should complement her attire in style, size and colour. For second-time brides, popular alternatives to the traditional bouquets include posies and single flowers. A corsage is appropriate for a simple ceremony where the bride wears a suit or a dress. Baskets of flowers and elaborate arrangements are more appropriate for younger brides.

ARRANGEMENTS

Flower arrangements for the ceremony and reception venues depend on the size and style of the buildings, regulations and the overall formality of the wedding. Arrangements may also complement the attire of the bride, the maid or matron of honour and bridesmaids (if any).

CHOICE OF FLOWERS

There are some flowers which a second time bride might want to avoid because of their particular symbolism for first time brides:

Flowers generally	White	*Innocence*
Daisy		*Innocence*
Lilac	White	*Youthful innocence*
Lily	White	*Purity*
Orange Blossom		*Chastity, fertility, virginity,*
		Your purity equals your loveliness

Until the middle of this century it was thought essential for first-time brides to carry bouquets of white flowers and wear orange blossom, but now almost anything is acceptable, and for both first and second weddings even garden or wild flowers are a valid choice as long as they reflect the mood of the occasion. Seasonal flowers are a good choice and often cost less too.

BUTTONHOLES

Buttonholes for the principal men of the wedding party are normally white carnations and as for first weddings, the groom generally wears a different colour.

FLOWERS

Florist

Address

Telephone

General flower style

General colour choice

	Colour	*Style/Shape*
BOUQUETS		
FLOWERS (Headdress)		
BUTTONHOLES		
ARRANGEMENTS		
Church		
Altar		
Aisles (pew ends)		
Reception		
Tables		
Cake		

TOTAL £

Flowers	No.	Delivery/Collection	£

CHAPTER 17

Wedding Gifts

A bride's trousseau refers to the items she takes with her to start her new life, for example, household linens. Today couples tend to buy such things together, have them already either personally or from a previous marriage, or receive them as wedding gifts. The essential new items for a second-time bride are her wedding dress, her going-away attire and night wear for the honeymoon.

If the bride has been married before, she will presumably already have many household items that normally appear on a gift list and although the bride and groom may feel that they do not need traditional wedding gifts, they may be surprised to learn that many relatives and close friends may want to give gifts in order to contribute in some way and others may feel awkward not giving a gift so will send one anyway.

Although it is unusual, it is permissible to include, 'No gifts, please' on the invitations. Many people will honour the request but some will donate gifts despite all efforts and if they do, gifts must be accepted graciously.

From a guest's point of view, the size or elaborateness of the wedding should have nothing to do with the amount of money spent or given but on affection for the couple and financial ability. Some more unusual gift ideas the guests might like to consider include:

Tickets to events;
Season tickets to sports, musical or theatrical events;
Gift vouchers;
Games;
Holiday equipment;
Hobby items;
A year's supply of specialities such as wines, fruits or flowers, delivered at specified intervals;
Leisure equipment may be given by a group of relatives or friends;
Membership to clubs;
Subscriptions to publications of interest;
Personal, household and vehicle security devices and systems.

If the prospective bride and groom have been living together and the invitations are sent by them, gifts should be addressed and sent to the bride and not to her mother.

Thank-you letters should be sent on the day that the gifts arrive, if possible. The groom may share the task, especially when the letters are for his relatives and friends who may be unfamiliar to the bride. Thank-you letters should be personally handwritten and not printed.

CHAPTER 18

Parties

PRE-WEDDING

Engagement

Naturally, engagement parties are in order and are a time to share the happiness with relatives and close friends. A party for a young prospective bride may still be given by her parents. A party for an older couple with grown children could be given by the bride's children. The announcement and toast at the party could be made by the host. Obviously, no reference must be made to any previous marriage of either member of the couple.

Engagement gifts are generally given only by relatives and close friends and are more often given to first-time brides. The gifts should not be taken to an engagement party since they are not expected and may embarrass those guests who have either not made a purchase or have not brought it with them. If given, they should be sent or given to the prospective bride in advance.

Social

It is traditional for the groom's mother to call the bride's mother to express her happiness at the news and to suggest a dinner party. For a second marriage, the bride and groom may feel that they should arrange this themselves, hosting a small dinner party and including any immediate family members to give them a chance to meet and socialise before the wedding.

Shower

If the bride has long-standing friends who attended the first shower, it would be better for the bride to reject the offer of a shower now to which invitees would feel obliged to donate a gift. If, however, the bride has new friends who were not part of her first wedding, then a shower would not be inappropriate. It is necessary to send thank-you notes only to those guests who were not present at the shower; if the bride personally thanks those in attendance as the gifts are unwrapped, she need do no more.

It is not really proper for members of the immediate family to give the shower. Alternative pre-wedding get-togethers in the bride's honour to which guests are not expected to donate gifts are luncheons, teas and cocktail parties.

Rehearsal Party

There is no reason why a couple should not hold a party or dinner for the wedding party following the ceremony rehearsal (if there is one) as it is an enjoyable way to share some time with the principal people during a very busy period and to exchange wedding gifts.

The rehearsal party is normally the responsibility of the groom's family.

Hen and Stag Nights

There is no reason to feel uncomfortable about sharing happiness with family and friends and including children provided that the occasion is suitable for their ages.

POST-WEDDING

It is a polite gesture to entertain both sets of parents and then the best man, maid or matron of honour and any other attendants after the wedding when the main festivities are over.

The good advice for first wedding applies equally to hen and stag nights which precede second weddings. The celebrations traditionally held on the eve of the wedding now take place some days before, allowing a time lapse for recovery!

Depending on the wishes of the prospective bride and groom, the party could be a small group of close relatives and/or friends going for a meal.

For a first wedding, the responsibility for arrangements would fall upon the chief bridesmaid but for a second wedding, the prospective bride and groom may wish to make their own arrangements.

CHAPTER 19

The Day

The following pages may be used for planning a timetable for the wedding day.

TIMETABLE

Time	Programme	Notes

TIMETABLE *continued*

Time	Programme	Notes

TIMETABLE *continued*

Time	Programme	Notes

CHAPTER 20

Afterwards

fter the wedding and honeymoon, there is the matter of tying up loose ends.

ATTIRE

Hired attire must be returned.

THANK-YOU LETTERS

After the honeymoon, it is the bride's duty to write and thank those who gave gifts. It is acceptable for these to be sent after the honeymoon but they must be sent as soon as she takes up residence in her new home.

DOCUMENTATION

Wills

It is worth paying a fee to a solicitor to ensure that wills are properly drawn up and contain no ambiguous wording. It can be an expensive and lengthy business resolving badly worded home-made wills.

Name Change

It is traditional for the bride to change her surname when she marries for which certain records will need to be amended. The following organisations should be in formed in writing:

DOCUMENTATION

	Date Done
School/s	
Employer	
Inland Revenue	
Department of Health	
Department of Social Security	
Electoral Roll	
Bank	
Credit Card Companies	
Building Societies	
Post Office Savings Accounts	
Premium Bond Office	
Insurance Companies	
DVLC	
Passport Office	
Doctor	
Dentist	
Clubs	
Associations	
Mail Order Catalogues	
Relatives	

DOCUMENTATION

	Date Done
Friends	
Others	

INDEX